Love's Wishbone

poems

Robert Pfeiffer

Plain View Press, LLC
1101 W 34th Street, STE 404

www.plainviewpress.com
Austin, TX 78705

Copyright © 2024 Robert Pfeiffer. All rights reserved under International and Pan-American Copyright Conventions. No part of this book may be reproduced or distributed in any form or by any means, or stored in a data base or retrieval system, without written permission from the author. All rights, including electronic, are reserved by the author and publisher.

ISBN: 978-1-63210-105-1
Library of Congress Control Number: 2023949241

Cover art: Photograph by Erin Ewing
Cover design by Pam Knight

We Find Healing In Existing Reality
Plain View Press is a 45-year-old issue-based literary publishing house. Our books result from artistic collaboration between writers, artists, and editors. Over the years we have become a far-flung community of humane and highly creative activists whose energies bring humanitarian enlightenment and hope to individuals and communities grappling with the major issues of our time—peace, justice, the environment, education and gender.

Love's Wishbone

poems

Robert Pfeiffer

Also by Robert Pfeiffer

Bend, Break

The Inexhaustible Before

for Layla

sweet girl,
you are absolutely everything

Contents

Midlife — 11

The Sense of Failure — 13

Redemption — 15
Elasticity — 16
A Solitary Life — 17
The Nobility of Practice — 18
The Sense of Failure — 19
In the Cut — 20
Behind the Skin of Clouds — 22
Rising — 23
Flicker — 25
How to Keep It Going — 26
Generalized Anxiety — 27
Social Anxiety — 28
Panic Attack — 29
A Common Cold — 30
Hands — 31

Dancing in the Morning — 33

Grownup Magic — 35
Selling the Condo — 36
Robin's Nest — 38
Coffee Spoons — 39
Dancing in the Morning — 40
Doing My Daughter's Hair — 41
Slow Burn — 42
The Girls Who Spend the Summers at the Beach
   Are the Gods of Time — 44
Skinny Dipping — 46
Her Virginity — 48
The Selfishness of Men — 49
All You Do Not Own — 50

The Long Thaw	52
Disappearances	54

The Great Dismantling — 57

Story Sonnet of Cocaine and Heartbreak	59
Ascension	60
Rorschach Days	62
Hospital Beds	64
After the Diagnosis	65
My Father in Waiting	66
The Great Dismantling	68
The Halls of Churches	69
What Hoop Heads Know	71
Ancient Medicine	72
Falling in Love With Water	73
Adult Swim	74

A Dream of Staying — 75

Six Feet	76
Driving With Layla	77
Summer Scene	79
Summer Storm	80
A Resurrection of Carpenter Bees	81
A Dream of Leaving	82
A Dream of Staying	84
Meditation and Despair at the Home Shrine	85
Mount San Jacinto	87
Taking Down the Tree	88
The End of the Holidays	89
The Last Full Moon of the Decade	91
Re-stringing My Guitar	92
My Daughter Playing Guitar	93
Only Child	94
The Heart Breaks Back	96
The Mystery of Your Darkness	97
Wounds	98

The Broken Tent   **99**
   Ars Poetica and the Bones Brigade   101
   Room 904   102
   Elegy for Phife Dawg   103
   Almost Running Over Maya Angelou on My Bicycle   104
   Blackface   105
   Opportunity   107
   The Broken Tent   108
   Roadkill #2   109
   Roadkill #3   110
   Degrees of Freedom   111
   Thoughts and Prayers   114
   Mediterranean Passage   115

Time and Distance   **117**
   A New World Order: Love Poem Number Whatever   119
   Resuscitation   120
   Taking a Nap With You   121
   Searching for Woodpeckers   122
   For Love of Birds   123
   Unprepared   125
   Time and Distance   126
   When it Rains   127
   Love's Wishbone   128
   To My Daughter in Her Sadness   129
   Buffet   130
   Epilogue   131

About the Author   133
Acknowledgements   134

Midlife

> *He knows every time this happens, he's moved just a little closer to the darkness outside.*
> James Baldwin, "Sonny's Blues"

I sit in the cavernous gymnastics center
as my daughter handsprings into evening.
Mid-November, when the air is finally clean
and dusk lays down the heavy sky early
with that unmistakable, pale melancholy.

From the viewing balcony, I see them all—
toddlers just learning to climb, all the way up
to teenagers who drove themselves here,
spinning their desperate bodies around the high bar.
And my daughter, somewhere in the middle,
now walking backwards down a balance beam.

It's loud, and a little too hot, and it smells
noticeably sour from the youthful exertion.
And I remember another gym, mid-winter,
me my daughter's age, after school,
waiting to be picked up, my friends and I,
careening like beautiful maniacs on scooter boards,
as outside, the wind plunged into night.

And now it's hard not to remember the way
the night air was almost too much,
too dense to breathe, when we'd emerge
after practice, ten hours after first period,
the basketball court deep beneath our school.
We'd emerge. Mornings dark. Evenings dark.
How dense and how new—to come up finally,
and see our young breath fly then fade
into the blackness before us as we fumbled
for the keys to start the cars to take us home.

Now, they call the classes to an end, and the girls
gather around for stickers and unicorn stamps,
and my daughter is all smiles as we walk out
into the night; leaves rattle in the parking lot.

I'm not going to worry about the seasons anymore.
They're ticking by too fast, accelerating as they go.
I push it all away again. We climb into the car.
It lingers—*how much of being an adult is hiding
the dark core from our children? How much?*

All we do is pretend everything is fine.
All we do is try to find a way forward.

"Are you crying, Daddy?" I hadn't noticed.
"I'm okay. I'm okay, Sweet Girl. It's nothing."

The Sense of Failure

Redemption

A poem is a prayer sent to the universe.
Sick of gods that don't listen,
we spin words into faith, find meaning
in the days that we are given.
There are thousands of prophets scribbling
benedictions on legal pads.
We believe in the life that can be—
that must always be enough.
Love is our religion; the world is our text.

The final line is attributed to the Sufi poet Rumi.

Elasticity

> *And you are still my daughter.*
> W.D. Snodgrass

You feel it stretching out from within—
not the minutes from the hours,
the long days and short years,
but rather, the leniency of your permission.

The first year, every breath observed
like a delicate experiment; then steps
toddled with arms buffering any fall,
backs bent, shuffling after her.

And later, you and your wife flank her,
and lift her in your hands above the world,
over frozen puddles, onto chipped curbs,
until your arms and hearts can't take it anymore.

And in just a breath, you can't keep up,
and though you don't want to, you let her go
further ahead, until she rounds the corner.
Until she goes there without you

and comes back someone else—
a whole person manifesting from the ether—
a young woman at eight—all opinions
and attitude and jokes and miracles.

And instead of coming to you in hunger,
with skinned knees, or a battery of questions
you forgot the answers to decades ago,
she comes to you with friends and plans.

And guilt grows inside you like cancer—
frustration and regret, your fucking temper,
predictable but tragic. She still loves you,
but you'll never forgive yourself.

And she's running into the years now,
and you can't see where she's headed,
and you try to hold on; you try to pull back,
and the tether is old and worn. But unbroken.

A Solitary Life

I only want work I can do alone—
give me the cold blank page, the empty room;
give me space to practice and fail and fail—
dark window boxes, frosted glass, quiet
except for the hum and clank of the heater,
the occasional car horn or gun shot.
Maybe the drone of cicadas outside, owl call,
coyote howl, or wind through the tall trees.

Keep your suggestions to yourself, thank you.
I'm convincing myself that this matters—
still—digging silently, like an earthworm,
eating dirt, gathering materials
for survival. You cannot help me now.
I've tunneled much too far to give a fuck.

The Nobility of Practice

You need to have practiced, to have apprenticed,
for 10,000 hours before you get good.
　　　　　Malcolm Gladwell, *The Outliers*

I love thinking about people, alone,
in their rooms, hunched over a notepad,
a guitar, dancing in front of a mirror
with no one to see the incremental progress,
unnoticeable, really. So, it's by blind faith alone,
or a nearly-psychotic dedication to craft
that anyone ever gets good at anything.
Yes, there are geniuses—meant to do
that thing they've found—they burn bright,
phosphorescent humans walking among us.
But it's a mistake to think you are one,
or to assume they don't also work like mules.
Windowpanes grow dark; the room stays bright.
Broadway dancers sweat through their clothes
seven nights a week, practicing long after
the world has headed home for the evening.
While most lean back, kick off their shoes,
they breathe deep on the balls of brutalized feet,
interlock their fingers, twist their arms outward,
stare like lions and crack their knuckles.

The Sense of Failure

When I'm feeling particularly worthless—
when the bank account is low,
and the house needs work I can't do,
when I catch myself in the mirror,
bags under my eyes like puffed bruises,
when all the promise so many promised
I had seems quite clearly pissed away—

I can sometimes remember that night,
saying goodbye to my first love,
off to college the next morning,
she dabbed my cologne on the hood
of her favorite sweatshirt and held
it to her nose, her eyes watering,
and pulled me to her soft lips.

And I can only sometimes think
of how my wife, my life's love,
always sleeps on my side of the bed
when I'm out of town for the night,
getting as close to the ghost of me
as she can, as if even in absence,
I make her feel safe and warm.

Every now and then, I can draw
to the front of my mind my daughter,
her feet kneading my side as we sit
on the couch, cartoons on the tv,
the sound of her whispers, the feel
of her tiny arms encircling my neck,
the weight of her on my shoulders.

I can pull myself out, only sometimes.
And remember that on my best days,
I am something worth being missed.

In the Cut

Do you always remember the first notes—
the ones where you had no clue what to do,
and still didn't care, banging the neck into doorframes,
clanging metallic notes off the fretboard?
Standing there on stage, can you still feel the moment
it clicked—a square peg finally into a square hole?

When I see you laying back in the cut,
between the implacably cool keyboardist,
and the fervent, point-of-the-arrow drummer,
I think enviously of your ten thousand hours,
and the ten thousand that preceded those.

I imagine you slumped over on the edge
of your single bed in your parents' house—
the brittle shell of your four walls
the only thing between you and the chasm
of suburbia you felt you needed to hate.

You skipped the lessons and kept to yourself,
racing to get through your first Marley tune—
a simple, three-chord progression you could play
almost right away, and did over and over and over
and after a week, *goddamn* the bass sounded good!

Eventually, there were a couple groups,
runner up in Battle of the Bands junior year.
Nothing to indicate the world to come.

You eschewed the party life in college
for the rigorous, oft-stoned practice time
you shared only with yourself and your pet cat
whose disinterest seemed a daily affirmation.

You dropped your Bio major for Music Theory
and your dad hit the roof, but he didn't get it.
He didn't know you had inside of you
a certainty in pursuit of the muse, the music,
that he didn't know existed inside of men.
He didn't understand that when you heard Miles
it was like boiling water poured on your brain,
and there would be no going back again.

Then the frozen hours—I imagine you for years
inside your walk-up apartment, running scales,
messing with effects, eyes closed around a groove
like meditation—you sought the peace you found.

I want to know if, standing there now, you remember
what it was like when you first looped the strap
over your shoulder, plugged in, and plucked a string.
As your hand slides over the instrument like a squid,
and your shoulders are slumped in perfect nonchalance,
a half smile and a subtle head nod, do you remember
what it was like when you didn't know how to play,
when it was all new and nothing came out right?
What was it like when you had to think of the next note,
before it became, for you, as natural as breathing,
became, for you, as simple as the night sky spilling rain?

Behind the Skin of Clouds

Look at the way the TV hangs over the mantel;
there could be a fire burning, but tonight, there is not.
The staircase turns and climbs towards the bedrooms;
your wife and daughter are quietly drifting off.
Night has come on; the windows are black—
outside, the animals hunt or hide, as they must.

Soon, you too, will crawl into bed, try to forget
yet another disappointing day, more regret, more shame.
You kick off your shoes and socks, open a beer,
lean back, put your palm to your forehead and wait
with the lamplight and cicada song, for what?
Some success you always assumed you would have?

Take a long pull. Remember the game at St. Mary's.
10 years old. Cold night, gym lit like a hive.
The championship. Parents lining the track above.
"Just do your best. That's all you can ever do."
You repeated your father's words like a mantra
the whole walk home, your shot at the buzzer a brick.

You tried; you failed. You deflated onto the court.
You had let everyone down for the first time.
It sticks with you. Even now, you replay the scene—
the ball in slow motion, clanging off the back rim,
arcing to the floor, J.P. putting his hands on his head;
Kahlil, who wanted the last shot, turning away.

What's the point these ceaseless trips into the past?
There are better ways to spend what time you have left.
Three decades and six thousand miles, and still
you worry that you should have passed instead.
All your goddamned failures, like water torture,
nagging at your sleeve, pulling you backwards.

Outside, the sickle moon hangs behind a skin of clouds.
In the gumtree, the squirrels sleep under the eye of the owl.
Upstairs, your family moves through dreams of love
and here you are, thinking only of some boxcar of words
that could bring you into the now you've been missing.
You've got to find a way to believe you've already won.

Rising

The first of many—
a kid named Jay.
Didn't know him well.
Drove hopped up.
Hopped curb, wet grass,
launched into tree.
Backseat passenger,
ruptured, crawled
hours for help,
saved the third;
too late for Jay.

Went to the funeral
in that elegant church.
Remember his friends,
caught between
sorrow and celebration.
Catatonic mother.
Young brother
tugging at the hem
of his father's suit.
Went to pay respects,
to support friends,
but also, went to feel
something grave,
to touch cold reality.
They released balloons
in his school's colors,
towards the heavens.
My shame rose too.

My daughter loves
balloons. Always has.
When she was a baby,
we would tie them
to her wrist in a bow.
Her eyes would follow,
rising, astonished.
Then, a kind of game
keeping one in the air,

the closer to the floor
the better, cackling
at the challenge she made.
Now: water balloons—
full wind up and release,
the cool rush bursting
across hot summer shirts.

She is rising now too—
through years of schooling,
through dress sizes.
The years slide by on rails,
not fast enough for her.
But I am so fragile now.
Softened by inevitability.
A single hard fall
could shatter what remains
like a skein of ice.
All I want is quiet
evenings, the smell
of sauteed garlic and onions.
at dinner time.
No more danger.
No more razor-line dreams.
All I want is soft landings
for the small handful
of people I care about
still here.

Flicker

> *And would it have been worth it, after all...*
> T.S. Eliot

You wake in the middle of the cold night,
not with a start, like when you were a child
and had snuck a horror movie or two,
but with an emergence into terror.
You lay in bed, shift sides, flip your pillow,
try everything you know—white noise, whale calls—
before it's too late and you just give up,
head downstairs, make coffee, and scroll the news.
It's just Tuesday—same shit, day in, day out.
Ceiling white and smooth. Headlights prowl outside,
slide over the bed. There is no comfort.
Your wife moans. You wish you could've done better.
You hope it's enough. Try to breathe. Lay down
your dreams. You were never meant for greatness.

How to Keep It Going

I think from time to time it's probably best
to imagine your wife at the landing
on the stairs asking you for a divorce.
Severe, there, at the end of her silence,
hands on the bannister, a long exhale,
as beautiful as the day you met her.
Picture her there, with nothing left to give,
and you, on the couch, digging for the words
to make her believe you still have inside,
buried under all the years and heartache,
all that's slipped away, that thing she once saw.
But all you have is words; if you somehow
could put the right ones in the right order,
you could make her believe in forever.

Generalized Anxiety

Because someone has to worry about everything,
I'm up, again, in the middle of the night.
The air conditioning clicks on. The fan spins.
A car thunkthunks over the manhole cover out front.
Who is behind the wheel at quarter past three?
At least there is motion. Stasis is death,
or at least, that's what someone once said.
The wind picks up, rattles the windows—
that dead pine tree in the neighbor's yard
is probably listing at a terrifying angle.
The neighbor whose son's name I got wrong
six months ago, twice, after knowing him two years.
His son who went missing for a couple hours
last fall, who's sneaker we found by the creek
and so, assumed the worst, until they found him
with his army men on the muddy bank
of the reservoir a half mile south.
And so now I lay awake and think
about human trafficking and parental negligence
and the world's long slide from innocence
and our daughter's cruel, irreversible spot in it.
And how, when the Georgia Pine does fall,
it will fall through their roof, and how
someone will have to come and chop it up
and grind it into a billion little pieces,
and how that tree is home to a family
of squirrels, and more insects than I can fathom,
and to all those little grackles, just now
beginning to signal the start of another day.

Social Anxiety

My wife cannot stop looking at her phone—
she sent a text hours ago, but no response.
Three dots waved like water then dissolved.
And now: the spiral. Unsure of so much,
she is certain she has done something wrong—
overstepped some social faux pas, wrong tone maybe,
certain somewhere people are talking about her.
She will hear no different despite what I say.
Next, her appetite disappears like confidence—
untouched kabab slipping toward inedible.
And now, all the wrong memories are swirling
through her as if caught on the wind.—
time loses meaning, and everything is *now* again.
A lifetime of misunderstandings, awkward silences,
imagined estrangements roil underneath her flesh.
Her eyes can't focus, her speech stammers.
She shrugs my hand from her shoulder.
It will be three hours before she clicks off
the light, sets her book on the bedside table.
But I know her sleep will be fits and starts,
the nocturnal blending of memory and reality.
And she will wake up tomorrow, the same
regrets pulling her like a coal-black tide.
And she will roll over and look at me, apologetic,
embarrassed, and still the best person I know.

Panic Attack

In the back of the ambulance
I held my wife close,
tried to hold her together,
to hold her here with me.
Blouse soaked through,
mascara running in rivers.
She thought she was dying—
stabbing in the chest,
couldn't draw a breath.
She thought she was dying
because she'd been killing herself
surely, slowly, for years,
a palmful at a time.
She counted down from five
through all her senses—
smelled no burning,
tasted no copper.
Saw me crying hard.
Heard our daughter's name.
Felt a reason to stay.

A Common Cold

I lay awake at night
amongst the discarded
carcasses of clotted tissues,
scattered cough-drop wrappers
littering the bedside table
and the carpet beneath,
NyQuil cup tipped on its side—
green sludge leaks slowly out.
I lay following the fan's path,
it's shadow on the ceiling
like a dream I can't remember,
just at the edge of vision.
I lay awake and think
of chicken and rice soup—
the porcelain bowl, the steam,
the sound of a metal spoon.
It was only a matter of time,
then. Time and rest.
Soon enough, never a doubt,
you'd be back outside,
with your friends, playing ball,
running through the days
like how only children can.
It was only a matter of time.
Now, every congested breath
is a prayer, desperate and dark.
I lay awake now and miss
every single thing, like fog—
dense and indecipherable—
half my life gone. If I'm lucky.
I slough off the comforter,
I make my way—floorboards
creaking a concert with my bones.
Flip the latch. Crack the window
just a little. A couple inches
makes all the difference.
The room needs some air—
February - fresh, cold, and clean.
Breathe. Let the night in.
Breathe. It'll be okay. Breathe.

Hands

My right hand is at twelve o'clock,
the wheel nestled underneath my wrist.
My left hand props up my head,
leaning on the driver's-side window.
Poor, unappreciated hands, unrecognizable
now, suddenly, it seems, in the blink of an eye,
dry, wrinkled, cracked, pale and splotchy,
no two ways about it—old-man hands.
The uneven, gnawed nails, half-moon cuticles.
How can it be that these hands, once soft,
wrapped around my father's index finger,
just like my daughter's would mine
thirty years later? Forty years later
I sit in rush hour traffic ticking off
brutality by the digit—the crooked pinky
broken during a playoff lacrosse game
senior year of high school and never set,
the misshaped index finger slammed in a car door,
and all the knuckles popped and engorged
from basketballs misjudged over the years.
I should have taken better care of them,
these hands that have felt so much,
have held so much I count as precious—
my wife's own hand as I slid on her ring,
my daughter, brand new and swaddled,
our dogs' faces, at their last exhale.
My whole life, whenever I was nervous,
I would tuck my hands into my pockets,
hidden from sight, to this day, I feel naked
without pockets, exposed to observant eyes.
These hands, which have built only poems
and Ikea furniture with varying degrees of success,
are now so old they look well used
though they have not been. There is nothing
much tangible they will leave behind
whenever I clench my fist and say goodbye.
I have clasped them in prayer when desperate,
but mostly I raise them towards the heaven
all around us when the breeze blows divine,
when the masses of swallows sweep

across the lake in a rapturous dance,
both palms on my forehead as I gasp,
trying to keep the universe within me.
Today, I pluck my middle-finger nail
with my thumb, clicking like a clock,
waiting at the light to turn towards home,
trying not to think about the stranger
who will one day soon, rest my hands,
one inside the other, forever, folded on my chest.

Dancing in the Morning

Grownup Magic

Once you found out that Santa was fake,
it was all over. The magic gone forever.
Still, you wanted to believe in something—
at ten, you made ten straight free throws
so you shot them the same way forever—
spin dribbledribbledribble spinbend&shoot.
Because for a while, sports were everything,
and you needed your dad's team to win,
you and your brother developed a complex
and ridiculous system of knocking on wood
for every game until the final buzzer.
You wanted so hard to believe in that power.
You'd press cold books to your forehead,
imagining that the stories would enter
with your deep breaths, because reading
was hard for you, and that broke your heart.
Later, you'd stare into your bathroom mirror,
conjure your first love's smooth face,
dream that if you just cared enough,
she would do the same—open a portal
between your eyes, and she would love you back.
It failed, all of it. Eventually. Obviously.
There is nothing to believe in like magic.
You are supposed to stop thinking about this—
it's the only way to function like a grownup.
Still, when you fear that life has already peaked,
when your mom's cancer prognosis worsens,
when your wife flies off all by herself,
when you're slipping from the razor's edge,
you need to believe in something more, again—
the words form in your mouth like a miracle
and you release them to the sky: *Please, God.*

Selling the Condo

Home is so sad. It stays as it was left.
Phillip Larkin

I sit on the hardwood floor,
my back against the cold wall
where a bookshelf used to be.
The furniture is gone. The pictures.

There is nothing left here
except the occasional dust bunny
as I wait for the repair man
to finish up with the dishwasher—

the last loose end before we close.
His drill whirrs; I barely notice.
No. I am too busy sitting here
trying to hold it all together.

It's approaching dusk in the city;
the windows are growing dark.
All over, families are sitting down
to dinner, but our home is empty.

Don't do it. Not again. Don't start
falling down the rabbit hole
of memories in this place. Breathe.
It's not worth it. Not now, anyway.

What would the repair man think
for Christ's sake? And yet, I wonder
sitting here on the hardwood floor,
my thumb tracing the chipped plank

where Layla held her Tonka Truck
high above her head, and smashed it
just to see if it would break—
what happens to them all?—

the memories from the life we're leaving.
Are they still here? Will they stay
rooted in the place they were formed,
or are they ours, alone, to keep?

They start to flash before me,
but I shake my head, catch myself
before it's too late, before
the lump in my throat is irreversible.

It's time to go. The work is done.
The hallway is longer than I remember.
I turn the key for the last time,
holding everything that fits, within me.

Robin's Nest

The first one was a flitting shadow—
a noise more than anything else.
Every time we would come or go,
she would flutter to the nearby trees,
then return to the nest above our door.

Soon enough, she was bringing worms
and grubs to the awaiting beaks,
outstretched, desperate, calling to her
across the breadth of their existence.
By summer they were gone.

The next spring, more robins came
and we felt it a blessing—full again—
the nest above the door to our home.
That was the hardest spring yet,
the sadness like a pall, but we made it.

And this year, another, thick breasted,
uneven, sliding her beak into the earth.
And when the cold front hit, she stayed
for the full week over her eggs—
delicate, cerulean—her little worlds.

Our daughter is eight, and shrinks
into her smile when she sees this.
She is innocent and fiercely moral.
She says she would never abandon them,
no matter how cold the world turned.

I think of all the years lost to cynicism,
but my heart was simply too small
to see the robins, and think of her
on her bike, peddling hard, auburn hair
buffeted by the speed of her leaving.

Coffee Spoons

> *I have measured my life...*
> T.S. Eliot

Only my wife's requires a spoon
to dissolve the single pack of sugar,
but it's not really about that, is it?
Just a little cream for mem, thanks.
Even so, I lift the spoon from hers,
dip it in my mug, stir twice,
clink the side three times,
leaving the milk spinning slowly—
a little mahogany hurricane.
Every morning for twenty years,
I have poured our coffee into
the mismatched eyes of our mugs—
hers burnt orange, mine pale beige—
which look up at me from the counter
begging for the warm release.
Every morning for twenty years,
I have carried hers in one hand,
mine in the other from the kitchen
to whatever room in whatever home,
and we have sat in the near silence
of morning, steam rising to our eyes.
The blackened pre-dawn windows
and only the sounds of our breathing
and the gentle setting down of mugs
has made it feel, so many times
as if the room we take our coffee in
has been the only room there is,
the only room that ever mattered,
rocketing together through nothing.
Every morning I hold the warm mug
in my palm, cream sweetens bitter,
and every morning she is there.
The whole universe could fall away,
and that would be fine by me.

Dancing in the Morning

Every morning, in our kitchen, we dance,
my wife and I, as we make breakfast,
spot-lit against the black pre-dawn windows,
our daughter watching cartoons from the couch.
My wife whisks eggs, pours them in a skillet,
I slide past, hand on her hip, fill glasses
with ice and orange juice, pull the hot toast,
scrape butter across it. We twirl around
one another, all habit and instinct.
Years ago, when this future was a dream,
we danced beside the crashing Pacific
under the full bloom of stars, my palm
on the small of her back, the universe
spinning us a song as we danced, danced, danced.

Doing My Daughter's Hair

She sits on the sofa, backlit
by the kitchen, almost a stranger,
the morning ink-black and foreign.
She eyes me with uncertainty,
her mother back to work for the first time
since she entered this world, gone
before she woke to beat traffic. It's only me
and this brush, and these rubber bands.

And, yes, this whole thing is so stupid—
there is no reason to feel this way—
of course, I've done her hair before,
made breakfast, picked out clothes,
but still there is a deep unease
to this morning, to my new duties.
We both feel it. The brush catches
in her hair, and she lets me know.
It catches again, and again
she lets me know and I flinch.
As I gather her hair in my hands,
sepia sliding through my fingertips,
I reach for the final loose strand
that has fallen to her lips,
and as I pull it towards the ponytail,
my finger catches her in her open eye.

And now she is doubled over
in real pain, real tears rushing,
like her future crashing down on me,
my palm covering my own mouth
praying for some early forgiveness,
my inadequacies swelling like a wave
in the black sea outside our windows.
Sweet Girl, I never meant to hurt you,
but I have, and we both know, I will again.

Slow Burn

Like an old friend, this evening,
the smell of a burned joint
on my fingers—floral and ash.

I am sitting on the back porch
with the fan on and the lights off,
fishhook moon through the trees.

The night awash with the sound
of crickets and cicadas; birds
I cannot name sing to one another.

The air is thick with August.
You went to bed hours ago,
our daughter, too, is asleep.

I am exposed, beneath it all
to this world as it finally is,
despite my own best intentions.

Yet again, I sit with only memory
and some kind of despair,
which coats me like sweat.

I light the roach, burn the hinge
of my thumb and index finger,
exhale into the sky above.

When I was young, life opened up
in countless paths. I never dreamt
that in the one I took I would be boring.

I miss how I must've once seemed to you—
dangerous, ecstatic, easily inspired;
I miss the adventures we could have had.

I flick the spent roach over the rail,
come in, lock the door behind me,
and climb up to bed, skipping over

certain floorboards so as not to wake you.
Behind me, throughout the night
the fan whirrs its circles for no one.

The Girls Who Spend the Summers at the Beach Are the Gods of Time

Hair curled by the salt air,
tans months in the making,
jean shorts and bikini tops,
puka shells and toe rings,
inside jokes and anklets—
those girls drove me wild.

We would visit the beach
for a long weekend, a week
some summers if we were lucky;
I'd spot them along the road
into town, walking and giggling,
sitting outside the pizza joint,
one head on another's shoulder,
worn out from the sand and sun.

They seemed to have all the time
in the world; we would leave
after breakfast on Sunday.
How could I compete with the life
they had then, in just a few days?
It was as if they already knew
those days would keep them warm
in memory's embrace forever,
when Eden fell away to life.

I would always be "just visiting,"
never quite fitting in,
never quite welcome,
our tides always out of synch.
They were always just out of reach
and I never got one for myself—
a whole puberty of disappointment,
the magic of their skin forever
troughed beyond the crest of a wave
that swelled and caught me inside.

But now, on the far side of 40,
I think of what they taught me—
of the irreversible vice grip
of those should-be golden days

Think of it now. Remember yourself
in the back seat of your parent's Saab,
crossing back over the bridge
out of town, heading home,
unchanged—still just yourself.
There will never be time enough
for all the dreams you may have.

And yet, even now, the sand is still soft,
and salt can fill the night air.
Can the breeze still come
through the dark, off the sea
reflecting the waning moon,
come like a girl's slender fingers,
up your neck, and tussle your hair?

Skinny Dipping

With varying degrees of nudity,
we would slide into the pool
at Penny Grant's parents' house,
when they were out of town,
keeping the noise down, the lights off
so the neighbors would mind their business;
and we'd drink beers and float
over to the edge to smoke joints,
and eventually we'd all be fully naked,
underwear in sloppy, wet piles
on the pool deck, our bodies just out of sight
with the extinguished pool lights,
but tantalizingly blurry under a black sky
and only a sliver of moon to light the yard.
Our young skin wet as heavy cream,
our floating was more than buoyancy—
somehow parallel to school and football,
field hockey and suburban Delaware—
the world opening up before us all.

Before me, the red-brown flash of nipples
cresting breasts of all sizes and shapes,
all terribly beautiful to me, all ethereal
and yet, an explosion of tactile imagination—
the tastes, the textures, so close, so possible,
the gateway to more and more and more.

And one night I remember draining my beer,
and setting the bottle on the rough edge,
my head spinning a bit, as I spun and saw
Yvonne Session, her face just above the water,
chin dripping, hair dark, bordering her jawline.
Her cat eyes smiled across the shallow end.
She made a perfect fountain of her lips and blew.

And though months later we would know
each other inside and out, I can never forget
the perfect arch of her body that night
as she swam a backflip with the grace of god—
not a trace of a blush on her cheeks,
only the white of her flesh, of her breasts,
then the shock of a tuft of hair—
all gone as soon as seen,
back under the surface, only for dreams.
The universe spinning outward forever—
so beautiful, so beautiful, so beautiful.

Her Virginity

If I tried hard enough,
I could probably remember
her breath on my neck,
the heat of its release
after the sudden wince,
the sharp sucking
through her teeth,
her muscles contracting
for a long beat before
she opened her soft eyes,
and smiled up at me,
at the weight lifting, finally,
from her beautiful shoulders.

The Selfishness of Men

Okay. Here we go. The truth
is that I didn't want a truce.
I wanted you to never fuck
another guy as long as you lived.
I never wanted you to be happy
unless your happiness was for me.
That was just something I said,
something to work in my favor.
And if I couldn't con you back,
I wanted your misery, like your body,
to be mine. I wanted your jealousy.
But you couldn't even give me that.
From birth, I was told that I deserved you,
was owed better than you, better than me.

All You Do Not Own

You'll never get it back.
Never nestle it gently within
your palms like a hatchling.

It's right there, always,
But *only* right there, like trying
to hold the water you swim in.

You know she was laughing
when she buried her face
into your neck and gently bit,

the last evening of high school.
There was a photo of it you took
to college, hung on your wall—

her brown shoulders, auburn hair.
you wrapping her tightly,
blowing cigar smoke into the night.

She was laughing the same laugh
you'd fallen for—like honey on a spoon—
rare, honest, from a well of joy unseen,

a place her father locked tightly
in ways she never discussed—
a shadow, always beside her.

You remember her, spot lit,
smiling in your passenger seat,
crossing the Delaware Memorial,

that great bridge between your lives.
But the sound of her laugh, inaccessible
now, and will be forever, it seems,

like swelling music from a violin,
locked in a thick black case,
and cast off the side of a ship.

Now, she's a Spanish teacher in Jersey,
tied to the land, her past, her family—
she's a mom, someone else's lover.

You hope she is happier now
than she ever dreamed she deserved.
Chances are, you'll never see her again.

Never hear her laugh, which kept you up
every night for a year, which you try
now, yet again, to bring up from the deep.

It belongs to them, and to the breeze
off the Jersey shore, to parts of the universe
that just don't care about you anymore.

The Long Thaw

I've hated her for half my life.
And before that, I loved her
so much it almost killed me. Twice.

It's been a long winter—no birds,
the wind unceasing, but unnoticed,
now. Hard earth under cold stones

under a raft of ice like a tomb.
Buried deep is the way my stomach
would turn on itself every time

something was even slightly off—
her disinterest over us like a pall,
and there was nothing I could do.

Deep, all that fucking embarrassment,
all those memories not fit for verse,
remarkable only to me. Buried.

If I could keep all that down there,
far away and forever, I would.
I don't want to see her again,

don't even want to hear that way
her voice would go all high and fast
when she'd get excited. Keep it.

But, buried there as well,
in a cast of dirt and ice,
is a part of me I miss—

something long-since calcified—
a joy like morning birdsong, free
from cynicism and the life-ache

I blamed on her, since that last goodbye,
years ago, which pulled the ripcord
on the whole thing—a small mercy.

But I saw her picture the other day,
holding her son, his first birthday,
and saw her smile, and felt nothing,

no dark cloud in my deep recesses.
Just a mother and her son—
a mutual love nothing to do with me,

and I smiled back, a grateful outsider.
Then felt some distant ice,
topping the hard earth, begin to soften.

Disappearances

No one deserves to disappear,
and yet Billy C. never came back
after his dad picked him up
after school on a Thursday in April.
In the sixth grade, the worst part
was that you'd never again use
the trampoline in his back yard,
and that you'd miss his vertical
on the court the following season.
In your 40s, you think about erasure.
One day the teacher picked him
to call roll in homeroom, the next,
his dad shows up for the first time ever
and the door to his Benz *thunked* shut
and he pulled away, taking a left
even though they lived to the right.
Think of Matt L., who let you stay
on his floor in the East Village
and watched you cross Lafayette
and head down into the Bleeker St. Station.
You never heard from him again.
Don S. walked into the darkness
after last call on Saturday morning,
following his pissed-off girlfriend.
I heard he's a lawyer in Chicago,
got alopecia and shaved his head,
but I haven't seen him since
he told us he'd catch the next cab.
Then, there are all the women
who were gone when I woke up;
there only ever remained the scent
of their shampoo on my pillow.
And there are more. So many more.
No one deserves to be forgotten.
No one deserves to disappear.
I remember when Magnolia Sharpe
was absent for a week sophomore year,
and the teachers were whispering

and the lunchroom was talking.
We heard something about her uncle
but no one explained it to us.
When she came back, she was translucent.
We could almost see the brick wall
she leaned against through her chest,
after the dismissal bell rang.
We joked and laughed, and she didn't.
We put a full page in the yearbook—
pictures of Magnolia playing field hockey,
singing in *Our Town*, smiling in math,
so we would remember her as she was,
before she was absent for that whole week,
before she started to fade away in front of us,
and long before that bottle of benzos disappeared
down her desperate and silenced throat.

*"No one deserves to be forgotten / No one deserves to disappear"
are taken from the song "Disappear" from the musical *Dear Evan Hansen*.

The Great Dismantling

Story Sonnet of Cocaine and Heartbreak

You became the whole city when I was young
and shattered, terrified you'd beat the odds,
astronomical though they were, sure
you were around every next corner, inside
every smoky bar—back when bars were smoky—
leaning on the bannister, talking to some guy,
unaware I'd come, about to ruin your night.
Again. And because the only place I felt safe—
certain of nothing else but your absence—
was on the couch, locked in my apartment,
I'd go out, my life a picaresque of parties
I wanted nothing to do with, and get high—
cut it up, roll a bill, up the nose, just because—
fuck it—weak plot, bad actors, boring story.

Ascension

Maybe I wanted to die.
Gassed on beer and weed,
enough coke to make anything
seem like a good idea—
we set out my first night
in Edinburgh, determined
to summit Arthur's Seat
in time for the sunrise.

We packed joints and cigarettes,
I strapped my acoustic
over my shoulder,
left everything else behind me,
on the other side
of the overnight train.

We walked through the alleys
of the city, silent and strange,
through the thick tall grass
of the ancient hillsides.
For hours, for years it seemed,
we climbed until we could see
the streetlight world below,
the subtle blade-edge of horizon.

But I couldn't catch my breath,
my heart thundering to panic,
sweat pouring down my neck.
My friends were too far gone,
I didn't want to put this on them,
so, I just laid down—*Fuck it*—
no one would understand anyway
just how much sense it would make.
He went out waiting for the sun.

I leaned into the far side
of a dark stone, closed my eyes
and tried to hold my breath.
I braced for the final spasm
in my chest, the one true cold.
But there was nothing,
then only the sauntering warmth
we had climbed towards.

Rorschach Days

You can't bring back the feeling,
but you know there were nights
as a child, when your bed was everything,
a whole world, and there was nothing
to worry about, so rest was possible.

Tonight, you sweated through the sheets
in the guest bed, just like last night.
Come to think of it, you can't remember
the last time your first waking thought
wasn't how many times you reached
into the freezer for the vodka.
How many ice-cold, thick swallows
did you sneak while no one was looking?

The mornings have been like Rorschachs—
ink-black and uncertain. The alarm,
the accounting for the night before—
did you fuck up, and how bad, like last week
when you fell into the wall at the landing,
breaking the framed picture of your family?
Soon enough, the shaking, the vertigo,
the need to try to fold into yourself.
You promise yourself just one sip before
you walk the dogs, one more before
you shower. Only one more before work.
There's a bottle in the middle drawer
of your office desk, safe behind a little lock.

You sit there, make yet another promise—
one fewer drinks tomorrow; start an hour later—
so many behind you already like shattered crystal.
You walk so slowly. You're afraid of everything—
afraid to look into the urinal and see blood,
afraid withdrawal could mean seizure, heart attack.

Yesterday, your wife showed you a drawing—
your daughter's image of you—red faced,
stick-figure arms raised like a werewolf's,
mouth open around your rage, temper ruptured.
It broke you clean, and though you know not to,
you went straight to the freezer—*Tomorrow. This time.*

At dinner, again, no one brings it up.
You all know what has to happen—
you *have* to get it together, or you will die.
After your wife and daughter go to bed,
you make another drink—stiff,
and try to focus on a movie. It is cold and smooth;
The sound of the ice clinking is still beautiful.
You pass out, wake up confused, like every night.
You climb upstairs, into the guest bed;
It's Tuesday, you have a meeting at eight.
your mind races as your body shuts down.

When you're a drunk, stoned, twenty-five-year-old
insomniac, there's a romance to the darkness,
a future as a writer, you imagine, as someone
who refuses to get beat down by this life.
But when you're steamrolling past forty,
and the ladder rungs turn slowly to sand,
it's dark-core terrifying. They don't tell you
the thoughts that fester in the night, alone
in your guest bed. Some sleep but no rest—
all the dreams you had to let fall away,
all your failures, personal and professional,
your aching joints and your racing heartrate.
You wrap yourself in the damp sheets,
torture yourself with amber memories.
Wonder if your wife cried herself to sleep again.
You wonder if your daughter will remember
you like this and nothing more. You wonder
if you're strong enough to save your own life.

Hospital Beds

Lying next to her husband in the hospital bed,
she cradles his favorite book in hard back,
whispering, almost, the words in case he's nodded off,
and softly flips each page with a single finger.
She feels the warmth from his narrow legs
under the sheet where they rub against her own.
His breath, a little sour, the same she's known
for fifty-three years, in the dark spaces,
in early mornings, and against all, she smiles.
She tilts her head and presses her lips to his scalp,
bald, creased by years, pocked with sunspots,
the crescent-moon birthmark she never knew he had
until the auburn's slow retreat of his early sixties.
And she remembers the smell of his pomade,
the way he would slide his fingers through it,
lost in thought, trying to solve some great riddle.
Remembers, too, a different hospital bed, different selves,
a child between them, kissing her head, smooth as innocence,
how the beeping monitor took over her heartbeat forever,
how he died for the first time the moment it went flat.

After the Diagnosis

I imagine him
after she's gone
to bed, sitting
in his old chair,
game on, mute,
lamp glowing
beside him,
book folded
in his lap.
How quiet
can a house get?

My Father in Waiting

I think of my father all alone—
all those years, all those countries,
waiting to board some flight or another
to take him from one foreign land
to another, from one meeting to another.
All those years alone and waiting
in any overly-lit, loud, plastic-chair
boarding area, or middle-of-the-night
silent with only the hollow tin voice
over the speaker making announcements
in Swahili, German, Portuguese, Thai,
and him, sloughing a hanging bag
onto his shoulder, wordlessly waiting,
extending his boarding pass at the gate.

I never knew how to imagine him
feeling. The grey suit, yes. The tie tugged
down a few inches, the top button open,
of course. But how he must have *felt*—
in all those concourses, all those middle seats,
all that recycled air all over the globe—
as foreign to me as his next landing.

He came home tired—short tempered,
frustrated, sometimes he'd fake interest
in our lives, sometimes he wouldn't.
We'd pretend not to notice, tread lightly.
So, I imagine he weathered the solitary
in anger, washed over. Washed out.
But now, I too know the relief of silence,
the release from family, so maybe
his exhales were long, unheard, and easy.

But when my brother left home, he changed—
a constant communicator since, relentless,
full of chitchat. And it gets on my last nerve,
myself a connoisseur of silence,
before breakfast, when he peppers me
with questions, unnecessary, kindling,
for small talk while my parents wait
for their lift to the airport, their flight home.

See they've been together for fifty years.
Can you imagine? Certainly, they couldn't
when he sat down behind her in History
sophomore year—sixty-eight. Upheaval.
The vast deserts of their life together,
the individual grains of conversation—
simply beyond their comprehension.

Beyond their comprehension, too,
that she will be leaving him soon—
when her prognosis takes its dire turn.
He is simply filling the final hours
while he can. Silence cannot be borne.
All this talk—he is doing the best he can
trying not to name his one, inscrutable fear.
I cannot imagine what he is feeling.

Hey Dad. Have a seat. Can we talk?

The Great Dismantling

When my mom was pregnant with my brother,
and then years later, again with me,
she gathered to her the things of the world—
stuffed bears, books with morals and happy endings,
she sewed blue and green patchwork blankets;
she sought out the things of soft landings,
brought them to her, and made our home.

And then we left home, and she got sick.
And now all those things are packed away in boxes,
kept forever, as if there were no other choice.
Then she got sick again—a final diagnosis—
just a matter of time. Time and comfort.

So now, she's begun The Great Dismantling.
selling the house, shedding the excess,
hasn't bought herself anything new in years.
No plans, no plans, no plans. Affairs in order.
We now approach, empty boxes in hands.

The Halls of Churches

Dear Lord, I want to believe
in order. I want to believe
in the possibility of peace
without rest. To keep going
without the sense that this hill
is getting steeper by the day.

Lord, I've been thinking a lot
lately of your churches—
thinking it's been too long,
save for weddings and funerals—
too long since I've felt
godly light with all its warmth
and promise of certainty.

Yes, Lord, I've been thinking,
not of sermons and baptisms,
but of pancake breakfasts,
of cleaning the local riverbed,
of stabbing trash with a stick
and chatting about something light
while children run and giggle.

Heavenly Mother, Father, Whoever,
last fall I voted for a future
in the belly of one of your churches—
my ballot cast, not my lot—
and it smelled of fresh coffee
and baked goods, an offering.
And there were framed pictures
from the 80's, childhoods like mine.
And it felt good, Lord,
like when the doctor cracks a joke.

I don't know if I'll be back, Lord—
it's only a thought at this point—
a sense of some shift forcing
out from beyond the veil.
There must come a calm,
or else there will come the break.
I pray only for the calm—
not asking a lot—only the calm,
the calm, the calm, Oh My Lord.

What Hoop Heads Know

They say if you hit just one good shot
on 18, it's enough to bring you back
to the course, dreaming of fairways and greens.
I don't play golf, but I get the idea.

If you shank three in a row into the drink
will the foursome of bankers behind you
sit patiently in their little golf cart,
or will they squeak their petulant horns?

Hoop Heads know something similar—
you never leave the court without draining
the last shot you take. It is accepted as ritual.
The lights come up as the sun goes down.

After your last run, you toe the free throw line,
lick your fingertips, take a few dribbles,
feel the leather pulse like a beating heart,
palm sweat from your brow, tuck, bend, flick.

At 8, you'd heave the ball from the hip, pray
you hit rim. Your prayers are smaller now.
Hoop Heads knows the deal. Keep shooting.
Stay till you make it. Nothing but net.

Ancient Medicine

We come to the ocean like patients
seeking some ancient, mystical treatment.
For a long weekend, once a year
we are believers in spiritual possibilities,
in the healing powers of water.
That wading in and surrendering yourself
to the currents can cure anything,
can somehow change the diagnosis.

We come to the ocean to listen—
to match our heartbeats to the sound of the waves
and breathe with the earth's music
until it somehow realigns us with our ancestors
who knew about these things.
Until it saves us from the lives we've got.
We imagine it hears us too,
understands the depths of our need.

We come to the ocean in pain,
and selfish in the way only we can be.
We claim every grain of sand
and the whole world to the bent horizon.
Like the tree that falls alone,
waves break while the world is asleep or gone.
All night they rise in blackness;
they never knew we were even here.

Falling in Love With Water

How boring it must be to go through life
and never fall in love with the movement of water.

The way off-shore wind blows back the breakers,
sending foam into the air like pulled cotton.

The way a swell can double up approaching a reef,
growing and leaning into its tidal charge.

How a river slides by over smooth stones,
or a lakeshore laps beneath the cicada song.

Study the perfection of water forming a glass,
forming the soft mouth that beckons it.

The way a single droplet moves deliciously
along the slope of your breasts, below your waist.

Adult Swim

> *Thoughts that do often lie too deep for tears.*
> William Wordsworth "Ode: Intimations of Immortality"

You emerge once more into the world,
lungs aching for air as you breathe deep,
let the water fall from your face.
A fog settles down; your eyes burn.
Your daughter cackles with joy, eyes clear
behind the tinted lenses of her goggles.
She's always been at home in the water, exultant—
couldn't even get her out of the bath as a baby—
she'd start shivering, lips veering to blue.
This is how you spend your summer,
while you still can. Soon enough,
she'll be here with her friends, worried
more about the depth of her tan
than with perfecting her cannonballs.
Today, four Adult Swims have come and gone—
your limbs are spent, but she is still happy.
The chlorine has done its work—
you close your eyes tight like a fever.
When you open them again, a chemical halo
encircles everything you see. Your daughter
swims once more into your arms.
One hand behind her knees, the other
at the small of her back, you bend and launch
her as high as you possibly can.
With nothing left to give, you watch her
rise, eyes widen, scream in laughter,
until she comes down, "apparelled in celestial light."

A Dream of Staying

Six Feet

The world has stopped,
and so, we walk the quiet
neighborhood over and over.

For some, for far too many,
it has ended alone,
convulsing behind closed doors.

A horror of the horror—
the gulf between their panic
and the crystalline birdsong

we discuss as we stroll—
my daughter skipping rope
along the way. Crickets churr.

The dog tugs its leash.
A breeze dusts the pollen.
There is hope for rain.

Driving With Layla

> *And you are still my daughter.*
> W.D. Snodgrass

Because there is nothing to do—
nothing open, nowhere safe to go—
our daughter and I cruise around
the south side of Atlanta, nodding
our heads to the music and chatting.
We are never really going anywhere—
no ETA, no plans, no destination.
So, we just drive around, the two of us.

We have been doing this so long now,
the earth we drive around on
has nearly completed a full lap
around the sun, which just now breaks
through the dusty clouds as we pass
Ebenezer Baptist Church, heading east.
Masked people on the sidewalks try to decide
whether to put their umbrellas away.

Our daughter is nine years old now—
one year and a whole world removed
from the normal childhood she knew.
By mid-April we needed a change—
she hadn't been out of the neighborhood
since early March, hadn't seen a friend,
hadn't smiled in just as long.
Her world was constricting around her.

So, she hopped in the back seat,
and we took a right then took a left,
and then the universe started sliding by
her window, and she unclenched her jaw.
We must've done this three hundred times
since then, at at least an hour a pop.
An amount of time unheard of before
time stretched out like a desert.

She would never have been up for this
until time with dad ran up against
pacing the living room for yet another day.
She controls the music, takes requests,
but ignores most of them. I am hip hop
and rock & roll. She is drum and bass.
She loves international DJs, so I've found,
and can "search 'em up" in a heartbeat.

She talks about normal kid stuff—
our dogs, video games, her favorite TV shows—
but her deep love for modern architecture
took me by surprise; solid colors, right angles,
floor-to-ceiling windows. She doesn't remember
that until she was three years old, we lived
high above the city in a modern condo.
Too late, I guess. She would love that now.

She would love a lot of things now—
things she can't have, things we can't give.
She's so patient though. She just doesn't know
what has been taken from her this year.
Doesn't know how short time really is.
How in 20 years she'll start missing everything.
The sideview mirror reminds me
that some things are closer than they seem.

In the rearview, she rolls down her window,
smiles into the breeze. Her hair billows,
and she tucks it back behind her ears,
closes her eyes and sings the chorus.
I double take at how old she is now,
the years are speeding up as the go.
She is falling farther away from me,
and I've never loved her more.

Summer Scene

The lifeguard stands are empty,
obscenely red against the sky.
The screams of laughter hushed;
the children have all gone home.
There is only the smell of rain
on the pool deck—petrichor—
no sunscreen or French fries,
The sound comes down thick,
is everywhere at once, like time.
The surface explodes from beneath,
millions of small, sharp bursts.
When the storm moves on,
the steam will rise upward
and start to fade into nothing,
and once again, we will wait for joy.

Summer Storm

It's that time of year
when the heat drags you to the bone—
the flowers give up and wilt,
and the lawn fades to sepia.
A tornado of gnats greats you
when you step into the morning soup.

It's been twenty years
since summer was all swimming pools
and catching lightning bugs,
and staying up late.
Later, pickup games at the park
and girls' smooth tan legs.

There is no leisure now—
you work all week long,
avoid the heat and mosquitoes.
You pray for October
as June unfurls before you.
By August, you're spent.

But this year, in the heart
of the sweltering hellscape,
it comes down like a summer storm—
heat lightning right to your core—
now, there are fewer summers to go
than there have been so far.

How much time have you wasted
worrying about the weather?
Your daughter is almost ten now.
Someday, if you are lucky,
she will say goodbye and tell
people the kind of man you were.

We are all dying at different speeds.
This much we know is true.
There is still time to make her proud.
Get off your ass—
we may never again be this close
to that fatal heat of the sun.

A Resurrection of Carpenter Bees

I thought it was only one—
crawling up and around
the back porch screens,
hovering a little, returning,
grasping in confusion
at the impossibility of escape.
And I did feel bad for it,
the gentle carpenter bee,
as I sat at the kitchen table,
finishing up a little work.
But the next time I looked,
there was second, then a third,
and I thought it was nice,
that they at least had company,
that I should open the door,
let them out into the world.
But then my little life
got in the way—something
small, seemingly necessary.
They slipped from my mind.
Several human hours passed
before I flipped the yellow leaves
of a legal pad, slid the cardboard
against the screen and the bee
clinked lifelessly into a glass.
I laid all three on the railing,
next to one another, expectant,
perhaps prayerful of some sign—
nothing. I turned away,
guilt bubbling somewhere inside.
Early that evening, I returned.
They were gone. Likely some terror
from above—a sharp beak,
an unseen wind—But just maybe,
in the absence of their captivity,
in the lightness of freedom,
one leg ticked from stillness,
then, after a long pause, wings beat
to translucence. Eventually all three
stumbled back into air. Once more
into the heavenly yellow of dusk.

A Dream of Leaving

I only ever dreamed of leaving.
My cul-de-sac'd childhood in Rockwood
was lovely, if only for a year or two
before we packed up and moved on, again.
We were always going, it seemed—
Sao Paulo, Tokyo, yo-yo-ing back and forth
between the States and the whole world.
But Rockwood seemed like ever after.
Our house was first on the right when the road
bubbled out like a cherry from its stem.
From our front porch, I could see the tracks
where each night, a freighter lumbered
around a hillside, the cone of headlight
vanishing along the dark track to somewhere.
And beyond that, the sound of the road—
cars rushing at all hours, the on-ramp to I-95—
Philly, New York, Boston—towering
smoke-shrouded cities from the movies.
From the furious pedals of my dirt bike,
I would look up on bright, clear days,
trying to stretch the depth of the sky.
I remember once, a jet flew overhead
low enough to see the individual ovals,
and behind each, a human on their way—
the aisle seats full, peanuts and sodas,
over patchwork fields, broad oceans,
banking into the magic of distant time zones.
And if I hopped the back fence my dad built,
past cattails and dwarf pampas into the woods
there was a creek I waded into up to my knees.
The water would flow east, towards the sunrise
that had already disappeared forever.
I'd stand there with my jeans pulled up
for what seemed like hours, listening
to the great cacophony of bugs and birds,
of cars and planes and trains, of children
screaming their way through games they invented.

The water would slide around my legs,
over smooth stones and, soon as seen, gone.
Once, alone, in late August, at dusk,
standing in the creek, the sound of geese
somewhere beyond the canopy of trees
I felt something and looked down—
a small leaf had floated on the current
into my calf, and before I could ignore it,
I saw a leaf-eating beetle in the center.
It was almost as though I was in the way.
So after a moment's hesitation, I bent down
and lifted the little craft to eye level.
The beetle ticked his legs at me, clear as day,
so I smiled, and set him back on the water.
And now, all these years later, I can still feel
the cool water on my legs, the slick stones
underfoot, the dusk air thick and humid,
can hear my mother calling me back home
from the window in the kitchen, can sense
an understanding moving in like fog—
there may be nowhere better to get to,
but you can always go there, just in case.

A Dream of Staying

In my dream, we were parting
before we met. You were saying goodbye
the same way other girls have said goodbye,
pretending it wasn't for forever—
to make it easier on me, easier for you.
It was humid, the end of the semester—
you, headed back to your hometown,
me, wanting only to follow.
The summer distance would never end.
You were solemn, but relieved.
I felt hollowed to my spleen.
You were keeping busy, small tasks—
organizing papers, zipping bags—
You didn't want to address the weight
of the future we wouldn't have.

Then I woke up—our bed, our home,
and realization opened up before me
like a field from deep forest.
We would not meet until years after
the dream's plot could've been.
I released the long breath
I didn't know I was holding,
pulling myself from the dream
which stuck like crude in feathers.
I turned to you and prayed it's true—
you're still here today. Still mine.

My wife, I remember that field
where we walked down the mountain
to the stables, grass frosted,
crunching beneath our feet,
our daughter toddling between us,
uneven, amazed, and every living thing
in the living world seemed
a moment in our lives together.

I reached my hand to yours,
rubbed your palm with my thumb.
My wife. My love. Let's stay.

Meditation and Despair at the Home Shrine

My office is a shrine to my family—
my wife and daughter are everywhere—
on the wall, leaning in frames on the desk,
dozens of loose shots and photobooth strips
taped up all around. Amniotic, therapeutic
for those days when the work piles up,
when nothing seems like it's good enough.

I've always wanted to be a dad.
Fell in love, got married. And we tried
and failed. For years. We saw doctors.
There were syringes, steroids, false starts,
dashed hopes, long weekends saying goodbye
to the children we never got to meet.
Then finally she came, and the world tilted.

Eventually we tried again. And failed.
Tried and failed. No doctors this time.
More heartache, though. More goodbyes.
Enough is enough. Our team is three.
I scan my walls and see the strength
of that number. Smiles through the years—
the only thing that matters—me and my girls.

But these are places I can't go back to.
Not really. And I crack sometimes
when I see her swaddled in soft cotton.
In one, I hold her under her arms
as uncertain feet struggle for balance,
and I can smell her baby lotion,
and feel her hair caught in my stubble.

But it's only for a moment, then it's gone.
I think sometimes I'd rather not remember at all.
I wish that I could shut my heart off,
like that digital picture frame on the bookshelf
across from my desk, power cord hanging limp.
I would get lost scrolling through her first years,
but it was too much. It sits, now, screen black.

But the frame next to it, a Father's Day gift,
says I am "Hands Down the Best Dad Ever."
In it, I hold her once more in my arms
on top of a desert mountain in California;
it is the day before her fifth birthday.
The air is hot and dry, and smells of pine
and dust, and of her old shampoo.

I'll never run it back. Never live it again.
Me and my girls. Repeat it like a mantra.
The sky is turning the color of a bruise.
Breathe. They say you'll miss today
if you miss yesterday too much.
Right now, my office is dead silent;
my daughter is out back shooting hoops.

Mount San Jacinto

Returning to earth is the hardest part.
The gondola, released from its high platform
drops, then swings nauseatingly over the gulf.
We pick up speed, sliding above the slope—
my daughter laughs and bounces a little;
I put a sweaty palm on her shoulder.

The world below is shades unforgiving
desert down into Coachella Valley
from San Jacinto, pocked with rough bushes
and jagged cacti. The horizon rises
slowly, waving in the seething heat.
We rumble over mooring poles. I shudder.

Trusting, we fall, according to some plan—
holding tight, hoping only for a soft landing.

Taking Down the Tree

Piece by piece you approach and disrobe her—
pull the ornaments from the brittle pine
by their metal hooks, their thistle strings.
You fold them in newspaper, bubble wrap
for your mother-in-law's porcelain star.
Back into their tattered, duct-taped boxes,
up into the attic for another year.
And she stands before you, exposed,
naked in that way you had forgotten.
Forgotten, too, how she blocked the sunlight,
crept in, a tightening in the room. But now
you can't remember the home without her.
And still, you lay her, prone, on the curb,
and sweep the needles from your hardwood floor.

The End of the Holidays

When you reach midlife, you mark every event with thanks,
or, at least, you try. So, each Christmas is a rebirth,
if only for a little while. Until the luster fades.

Even lugging the tree and ornaments from the attic
takes on the tone of a religious encounter. Give thanks.

You made it back up here with the insect corpses,
cobwebs, and insulation like cotton candy, like the snow
which has only fallen as dust once in the last few years.

And when the whole thing is over, the season a wrap,
you need to fight the fear that there won't be another.

As if you worship the ritual, you remove the ornaments,
wrap them in newspaper and lay them softly down
in the translucent plastic boxes which seal and lock,
protecting the decorations through the whole year.

When you decorate, there is music—joyous and loud;
when you take it all down, it is silent like a church
after the bible is shut tight—a funeral procession.

You shuffle upstairs with the boxes in your arms,
pull the chord, the door drops dust and cricket's legs.

You make your way up a single step at a time,
over and over, and stack the boxes near the wedge
of floor and ceiling, knowing they won't be needed
again until the seasons have circled once more around.

As you descend, and prepare to close the door
your daughter's toothless smile, her eyes glistening
with disbelief and that weightless joy of youth,
her new bike wheeled into view, rises inside you.

You take a deep breath, and one last look around;
a face smiles out at you from the aqua blue container,
out-of-date perm, shoulder pads, the paper yellowing.

A delicate ornament wrapped in an obituary—
"Susan 'Suzie' Horowitz of Dahlonega, Georgia,"
beloved mother, wife, and friend, dead at fifty-eight
of natural causes, service on Sunday, send flowers, etc., etc.,
now buried forever in our attic with memories and old clothes.

The Last Full Moon of the Decade

It's the last full moon of the decade,
and I just want to be left alone
more than anything. I do not feel
myself changing into something of note.
I do not feel anything but older.
The moon waxes, is full for a night,
then wanes to nothing again. This morning
it hangs over my neighbors' house,
my dog tugging at the end of her leash,
grey clouds like pulled cotton across the sky,
breath hanging on at the end of a sigh,
predawn, the decade drawing its curtain.
Take a bow. Kiss your wife. Hug your kid.
Write about it. Get to work. Get off your ass.

Re-stringing My Guitar

Relegated for a year to the corner
behind my desk, high-E sprung
like an untamed curl, a silvery lock
that would sing against the other strings,
tick against your amber body,
your coffee neck, when moved
by forces unseen, a stirring in the room.
Then, for another year, same spot,
naked, unable, disrobed, unstrung.

Old friend, I've neglected you too long.
I lift your light shell to my face,
inhale the sweaty metal of fretboard,
the musk of your mahogany hollow.
You settle your hip onto my thigh—
that's right. It's so quiet in this room.
But I slide the low-E from its sleeve.
Between my fingers, I clasp and pull
the whisper of its rough length.

My Daughter Playing Guitar

She has not yet moved off of high-E,
only playing a total of three notes
in various rhythms, orders, sure,
and even though every third one
clangs metallically off the fretboard
to my ears, the music is wonderous.

It's not the music that she makes,
but the way she sits on the couch,
legs crossed casually at the knee,
the body nestled into the hip joint,
looking like she's been playing
for longer than she's been alive.

It's the way she pinches the pick
between her thumb and index finger
then uses her middle to brush back
her hair from her unblinking eyes,
the notes conscribed in her songbook,
splayed on the stand in front of her.

It's the way she is trying to learn
something beautiful in her young life,
something that might sustain her
years down the road when I am gone,
when I cannot tell her it will be okay
and brush her hair back myself.

She is building up calluses on the tips
of her fingers to make playing less painful.
And playing is what makes the world
less painful. Another note clangs sharp.
It's not the music that she makes,
it's that, mercifully, she can make music.

Only Child

To be clear, you are more than more than enough.

But today, from across the trampoline park
I take you to every weekend to play, to watch

the easy joy of your back flips and aerials,
which leave the other parents at a loss for words,

and even teenagers raise their plucked eyebrows
in disbelief at you, all of an amazing seven—

today, you are trying to cross the rope bridge
which swings wildly above the foam ball pit

as your body weight shifts from side to side.
And the further you crawl out, the worse it gets.

And unlike all the kids that have gone before you,
you have no one holding the near end steady

against the chaos before the knot on the far wall.
And you seem to look back at the no one that is there.

On your own, you reach for the next rung, the next,
then slip, dangling beneath, before hooking a foot

over the side rope, pulling yourself up and through,
steadying your own self, catching your breath,

waiting for the rocking to calm before starting again
pulling with all you have towards the end.

And I jump up, lump in throat unnoticed until later,
and run over to you, past all the other kids—

the ones wiping their snotty noses with shirtsleeves,
the ones clutching their elbows and ankles,

wailing for their mommies or daddies, the ones
whose big brothers turn slowly away from them.

Following the vaguest of urges, I run to you,
past them all, even though I know,

and your lonely eyes tell me later, you know too,
that even if I timed the whole thing just right,

got my best bounce off the trampoline,
launched out headfirst over the void,

stretched out the arms that held you,
less than a minute in this world,

I could never catch your fall.

The Heart Breaks Back

Because her father never showed her love,
though he did love her,
she has never believed me,
though she knows I love her.

When I tell her of her beauty,
as I have a million times,
in ways big and small—
Tuesday mornings with coffee,

warm nights on the couch,
warmer nights breathing into her neck,
or her long asleep, whispering
into the night sky of our bedroom—

when I tell her of her beauty,
she'll smile sometimes,
and shake her head, telling me to shut up,
like it was just some joke.

And I'll see her in front of the mirror,
looking like an unfallen goddess,
But she'll turn this way and that,
pulling at parts of herself, and sigh.

She imagines tucking this, nipping that,
were it not for our daughter's eyes,
confused at her mother's tight glance,
her new and strange smile.

I tell her and I tell her and I tell her.
But still she leans into the mirror
to press away the lines
left behind by her wild and precious life,

and her heart will break back
through forty years of never feeling like enough.
Her heart will break back to a hug ungiven.
Back to words unspoken, her heart will break.

The Mystery of Your Darkness

You have been happy this last month, I think.
I think you have been happy here with us.
You jog in the mornings, then take a walk.
You listen to your music on the run,
then, listen to the morning, the birdsong,
the locusts' wings, the wind through the trees.
You move lightly now, it seems, almost free
from the yoke you lugged so long in silence.
So, when you go quiet now, as you do—
"radio silence"—I assume the worst.
You hate when I try to piece it together—
the mystery of your darkness, so instead
I lay in bed and pray it lifts with my words,
with your breath, and with the coming dawn.

Wounds

The wounds of your addiction—
like a shadow over a blind man—
make their presence known
out of nowhere, and hang over
the life you are trying to rebuild.

It casts itself over your home
with the murmur of phone calls
you take in the other room,
with any change in your eyes,
with a simple afternoon nap.

You are asleep beside her now,
but she can't tell you any of this,
because she knows what guilt can do.
So, she tries to discern from your breath
whether you are still there with her.

The Broken Tent

Ars Poetica and the Bones Brigade

> *The Bones Brigade was a skateboarding team in the 80's who often snuck onto people's property without permission in the colder months to skate in the empty swimming pools.*

He stands perched on the edge,
balanced, full weight on his back foot,
the whole board out over the chasm.

He pulls a breath into his lungs,
exhales halfway, and drops down
into the abandoned swimming pool.
The wheels race beneath him, a deep,
unmistakable sound against the plaster,
and as he approaches the bottom,
the board fishtails a little, and he knows
that if he falls, it's over; his body
has been broken so many times before,
but this time, he straightens, and pulls
his balance beneath him once again.

He sinks lower, into the deep end
where summer children do cannonballs,
and picks up more speed, eyes the high lip
and soon begins to rise back towards the surface,
and when the time is just perfect,
he pumps with his whole body
and pushes off the wall, into the air, flying,
free for the moment, and then flicks a foot
sending the board spinning and flipping—
once, twice, maybe three times.
He catches it as his body rotates.

At his highest point, as free as he's ever been,
he shifts his eyes back toward the bottom,
hoping only to stick the landing.

Room 904

After L.S.

It's alright.
        Leon Stokesbury, "Señor Wences and the Man in the Box"

Back when we were at our smartest—
dumb enough to believe any of this mattered,
could change lives, change the world,
we sat high above Atlanta in Room 904—
windowless in a building that burned
from within. We hoped it was worthwhile.

He hulked from his chair, dealing pain,
crunching Altoids, surly, a curmudgeon,
our teacher—a rhinoceros of wisdom.
Most wanted to hate him. Many did,
rooted firmly as he was in his ways,
his old beliefs about the greatest art.
Rooted like a thick-trunked oak,
a presence turned tradition on campus
casting shadows over the hillside.

Rooted to the things of this earth,
rising towards the unanswerable,
for years we perched like grackles—
flocks at a time, flitting, chirping,
making home for a season or two.
And when we left, no one noticed.
But then the winds came howling
through the branches of the oak
and it listed, finally, and never righted.

May we all understand how lucky
it all was, how changed we all were
after only a small season or two.

Elegy for Phife Dawg

> *Malik Taylor, aka "Phife Dawg" was a founding member of the legendary hip-hop group A Tribe Called Quest. He passed away on March 22, 2016.*

Growing up, they called me "Lil' Phife"—
the older kids did, "Phife" was my brother.
When he left home, I became "Phife Dawg."
It rang out in the hallways, the cafeteria,
from the bleachers at basketball games.
I checked "Award Tour" on my senior page:
"Phife Dawg's the name,
but on stage call me Dyno-mutt."
I shouldered that name with pride—
I even had it stitched into the front
of my black Carolina Starter Jacket—
I put my name on it—Phife Dawg.

But of course, it was never really mine.
I just wanted to be part of your tribe.
Middle school, high school, your voice
in my ears, your lyrics in my mouth,
drifting through youth, through suburbia,
spitting your bars over bass so loud
my parents could hear me from the street.
Just a white boy from Delaware—
not exactly your target audience. Regardless,
today, my windows down, my volume up,
I raise a glass to you, to my namesake,
to Beats, to Rhymes, and to *your* Life.

Almost Running Over Maya Angelou on My Bicycle

I was flying down the hill and came around
the corner thinking of no one but myself—
running late to my second ever course,
World Religions, my first week in college.
And from the corner of my eye, which was,
I confess, ticking the seconds of my watch,
I caught something leap, in body and voice
just in front of me, and I swerved, skidding
off the path and struck a lamppost hard
enough to check for damage to the bike,
to myself, then, finally, to the woman
who stood in exquisite linens opposite me.
My breath caught, a fish gulping air. She smiled.
"You know, life is too fast. Slow down, child."

Blackface

Ear to ear. You're smiling
like it's the funniest fucking thing
since Archie Bunker howled
"The Coons are coming," panicked
the new neighbors would toss
their watermelon rinds into the street.

And maybe it was just ignorance,
and not *Ignorance*—a lack,
simply, of knowledge or context,
that made you paint yourself up,
your face to match the natty afro,
the tattered, off-the-rack
plantation shirt. But I doubt it.
The benefit of the doubt is earned,

not a handout, like some other
"jokes" you no doubt partake in
when you feel safe, audience
known, assumed, bedsheet white.

Maybe it was "all in good fun"—
innocent in the way you imagine
your whole life to be, but I doubt it.

I doubt it like you no doubt
doubt the migratory shifts
of sharks in Middle Passage.
"Apocryphal" you say: how on earth
could the sharks have known
which ships to follow,
in which wakes would corpses
sink like shining stones?

You doubt there ever were fins—
any more than usual—slicing
through the surface, or unseen below.
You doubt language can be lethal.
You doubt anyone should get offended
at that picture, at your jokes—
"at worst," you say, "off color."

I doubt you'll ever get it—
the last of that shoe polish
from your lily-white skin,
even if you scrub it
down to the cold bone.

Opportunity

> *My battery is low, and it's getting dark.*
> The purported last transmission from NASA's Opportunity Mars Rover

Opportunity spun into nothing,
weary, mugged, wholly alone,
spent down to its solar core.

One final revolution, nothing
left to report. No more tests to run.
No samples left to collect.

34 million miles: so far to come,
motionless within her vessel,
slated for life only 90 days.

15 years, treads in the red dust,
scanning the horizon, isolated,
yet never a moment for herself.

The nobility of her silence—
unnoticed by the world she left,
distances too great to measure.

Her battery runs low—
she slows to a gravelly crawl,
the transmissions grow dim.

The planet spins. A final note.
Time to sign off, say farewell—
distant voices like kindly gods.

To care enough to call this love—
the earth winking in the distance,
mysterious, cerulean, finally silent.

The Broken Tent

Towards the close of 2019, massive brushfires devastated huge swaths of Austrailia.

Oh Lord Thou pluckest me out.
    T.S. Eliot

I cannot bring myself to write
about the fires—biblical, apocalyptic.
A land I've never seen, cinder and ash.
The size and scale, they say, unfathomable—
they transpose images over maps on the news
to get this American audience to comprehend.
To care. The whole east coast, they say
part of the southwestern deserts as well,
some of the Great Lakes burning like oil.
Satellites relay images from outer space—
smoke like ghosts haunt the bent edges
of the Earth. Some stories haunt me too.
I cannot bring myself to write about them.
Half a billion animals, they say, trapped
in a maze of flame, laid down eventually.
And this is the ledge I will not toe—
the point where I can simply go no further—
as the pitiless sun beat down on them,
through the coffin lid of smoke,
with not even the possibility of rain,
firefighters doubled over and wept
uncontrollably, as beyond their reach,
koalas howled their final inhuman agony.
For them, there was no word for "why,"
only the terrible bewilderment of "is."
The earth, though, She hates us,
and She should. She wants us gone.
And who could blame Her?

Roadkill #2

We are moving too fast to care,
coming or going—it doesn't matter
as long as we're behind the wheel,
or on the way—coming or going.
We probably don't even notice
their wreckage, scattered, smeared,
the lonely ghost of their bloodstain—
a whole existence in the truss of fur
we send shuddering with a blast
from our speed; on to other things
before we even see what we missed.
We fly past squirrels and birds,
shoulder relief at the deer caving
in someone else's fender, wince
at the dog who could've been our own.
But mostly, we roll up the window,
shift a little in our seat, adjust the air,
look for a better song on the radio.

Roadkill #3

I see you coming up the road,
sweating like a pig
on your morning run—
the humidity relentless,
the heat taking its toll
on us both.

I'm rotting where I fell,
after some strange clenching,
from a long branch,
in the middle of the night,
in the middle of the road.
You look away.

The closer you get to me,
the clearer your choice
to ignore me as best you can,
though I have tucked
my nose into my tail,
like your dog.

I've made you uncomfortable.
I can see it in the way you move,
trying not to breathe in
my terrible fragrance,
as all that I have ever been
drifts in air.

Keep running.
Do you care?
Dig deep.
Drifting. Drifting now.
Could you ever care?

Degrees of Freedom

> *Independence it may not be, but there are degrees of freedom left for those who see the fireworks in a fresh light.*
> Michael Holt's last Facebook post before opening fire in a hotel lobby and being killed by police.

I never imagined what it was like
to be you until you were shot dead.

Though we shared a fraternity, some friends,
we never really liked each other—politics mainly,

the chasm between us too great to bridge,
and neither of us cared to try, frankly.

And then I was done with you
for the better part of a decade,

until I saw you before a show in '09
and you hugged me like old friends

and I tried to peel away from you.
And that was that. And leads on to and.

Before it all went down, I watched you unspool,
from a 21st century distance, with no right

to make assumptions, no space to comment—
a stranger among friends among strangers.

My absence, my silence, I imagine
merely one of an unnoticed many.

And so, it was only after you strolled in
to the lobby of the Omni hotel, and murdered

that cabbie, getting his morning coffee,
after you aimed at the charging officers

and got what you wanted—a rage
of gunfire to send you from here,

pouring you out onto the marble floor,
that I finally imagined what it was like to be you,

in the dark hollow of the driver's seat,
the hotel across the quiet street, lit from within,

a gun in the back and a decision made.
And I think of your mania that night—

it must have been something
I'll never understand. I pray it was something

I will never understand. And I try
to imagine your smile the last time

I saw you. Imagine kindness in your voice,
warmth in your hug, and I walk right up

to the edge of feeling, for you, a sadness.
But then I think of Mr. Contreras,

of his family asleep in the dark hollow
of their home, of him leaving them behind

daily, cupping cold water in his rough palms
and splashing it over his face,

baptizing himself towards each new day.
And then I think of the terror spreading

through him when you approached,
realizing it wasn't a terrible joke after all.

And I wonder if you ever gave him
the chance to draw into his mind

some memory, some smile, some dream
from this world to take with him,

spinning in his head for his last breath,
something to keep your face

from being his last thread to this life.
And so now, I only wish you were brave—

brave enough to walk out alone
into your back yard, under stars,

take a last breath, and slide that barrel
into the dark hollow of your own mouth.

Thoughts and Prayers

> *What good is it, my brothers, if someone says he has faith but does not have works?*
> James 2:14

They treat it just like a game—
Hiding, but no Seeking.
Our daughter's kindergarten class,
crouching behind cabinets, in bathrooms,
the little spaces between classrooms,
beneath upper and lower-case letters,
chore boards, aspirations, class rules,
what empathy means to each of them.
They stay as quiet as they can
for as long as they can.
Teachers never call it what it is—
"A Lockdown Drill," they say.
"A Bad Man Drill," they say.

A week after the first one,
Layla was jumping on her trampoline,
when she stopped cold and looked
to her mom with a face I'd never seen.
What would the bad man want?
And in the silence between her parents,
our daughter read the whole thing.
And after some little lie,
aimed to keep her herself, for now,
she started jumping again, a little lower.

This morning, like every morning,
yellow light blooms from the dark
in kitchens where the breakfast tables
will always be missing one setting,
under bedrooms unslept in, again.

And this morning, like every morning,
lights come up in the Halls of Congress,
Halls which are, again, as silent as our daughter,
eyes tight shut, palms cupping her ears,
the thunderclaps growing nearer, nearer,
holding her tiny breath like a prayer.

Mediterranean Passage

From above, the empty raft roils
on the ink-black sea, the sun
still hours below the horizon.
Rain boils the surface like pestilence.
Six-year-old Yara treads water,
coughing from the fire in her lungs.
The current, an unseen hand,
pulls her from her mother and father.
Yara will never remember Aleppo
was golden while her parents beamed
as she wriggled like a fish in the sink—
her first bath, or how her brow creased
whenever she broke into tears.
Memory fails. Memory fails us all.
From the sea floor, we could see
they are falling like snow through night.

*"Yara" is a traditional Syrian name meaning "Water Lady."

Time and Distance

A New World Order: Love Poem Number Whatever

I ordered the southern fried chicken—
you had the salmon and roasted potatoes—
it was on the firm's dime after all,
your first day, meeting the new coworkers.

Your hair was parted and to your shoulders.

You had on a bright-red button down
and a knee-length black skirt I couldn't see
for the tablecloth and being polite.

Your eyes were the biggest I'd ever seen;
I was terrified you'd catch me staring.

We ate our lunch then went back to work;
I showed you the various shortcuts I knew,
the ins and outs, ways to lighten the load.

I wanted only for you to like me—
to be that thing you mentioned with a smile
when your roommate asked about your day.

Twenty years on, I still think about it all—
southern fried chicken and salmon,
black skirt, button down shocking red,
your cubicle adjacent to my own,
meeting in the copy room, the café,
at the coffee machine, cocktails after work.

Entry-level jobs, big city, late nights,
always making plans, always the butterflies,
the sense of falling into something new.

The two of us, growing into the two of us.

Your eyes were the biggest I'd ever seen,
like twin worlds, undiscovered and new,
like twin worlds orbiting one another.

Twin worlds to which I finally belonged.

Resuscitation

We need to fuck our way back to life—
let our fingers, our tongues lead us back
to how we once felt about it all.
It's slipping away one day at a time.
We are closer, now, to death than birth,
there's no two ways about it. And yet,
I can still slip myself back into that night
you crawled up the bed to my lips.
We've lived inside each other ever since.
The years are swelling, and we are dying.
My love, let me kiss you everywhere—
let me search for hope within, right now
and tomorrow, let me love every inch
until we have no more "Good Nights" left.

Taking a Nap With You

> *...which is why I'm telling you about it.*
> Frank O'Hara

There was a time
in what feels like a previous life
    when we stayed in bed
all weekend if we wanted to—
    before careers, parenthood.
We floated through our little universe
    at our leisure, together.
Then, once our Layla came along
    we'd lay her down
and slip again into the sheets
    together, midday, exhausted
beyond anything we'd ever known.
    But, as things do, the naps ended.
Years of domestic life, no stopping
    along the trail we tread.
Even so, more than all the gold
    sand beaches in the world,
more than steaming mugs of coffee
    on snowy mornings,
more than the crisp air itself
    swelling in my lungs,
I love those rare occasions
    when the house is empty
during the day, and we lie down
    on the couches to nap
a dog each nestled in the bend of our knees,
    we set a movie to quiet
and we slip from consciousness
    together, and return,
yes, return together once more
    in the warm afternoon light.
The ceiling fan circles like the years—
    one more trip around the sun.

Searching for Woodpeckers

The trilling comes down from the distant trees
through the bone-colored dawn and stops me cold.
The dogs' ears are peaked to the rapid tapping
which echoes hollow through the neighborhood
where I stand alone, my breath hanging fog.
Bacon cooking, Sunday papers still rolled,
laying in the front yards of the sleepy homes.
I stand deep in my silence, staring up
into the high branches of the Georgia Pines
looking for the bright red pileated head,
the shuddering of its movement like a piston,
beak needling tree-flesh, searching wormholes,
beetle-bores for grubs and morsels to survive.
The sound again. And again, I can't see
the living thing making that living sound.
And I think how nice it must be to live unseen
to burrow deeply, to excise truth like bark—
the work of digging becoming like a song
that drifts earthward from far-off places—
songs so stunning, they stop men in their tracks,
cause them to look off towards heaven and wait
for the dogs to get bored, tug at their leashes,
remind him that it's time to go home.

For Love of Birds

There is nothing new I could ever say
that has not already been said, and better.
And yet, I try, over and over again
to find new words to describe the feeling
when you see a red-tailed hawk slice the sky,
and ease into its perch atop the gumtree.
The sense that somehow what it leaves behind
is changed: silent, awed, a new shade of air.

The same when morning brings our aspen
full with a chime of wrens like ornaments,
or when pigeons drop from high windowsills,
arc through the city, deploy wings like chutes,
catch the wind, and waddle across the street,
or the one bard owl across the wooded park
who hoots for hours after the sun is up,
refusing the nocturnal blood in his veins.

Last year, they clear cut trees, and two red tails
stayed in our yard for a month, bewildered,
their calls bleating through the early mornings.
They hulked on our roof, on the bannister
of our back deck. The larger savaged the corpse
of a rabbit in our driveway. She called
to her mate, who carried it in its talons
high into the distance; an act of love.

Everyday we'd see them, like bright shadows
across the windows, could feel the wing beats
through the walls of our home, the walls of our chests.
It never got old, living with those hawks.
And I would dream of them in the dark—
of their deep-brown feathers, their razor beaks,
the speed of the beats of their bright-red hearts
and the ancient precision of their strikes.

My mother—a true believer in such things—
once told me that hawks are the messengers
from the spirit world, sent by loved ones,
to lead you towards peace and wisdom.
I don't know ... I've always been a cynic.
But sometime on a Tuesday in July,
they flew off for the last time—a new nest,
out of sight—and I have never been the same.

Unprepared

How does one cope with the drive home
on Tuesday when the clouds sag down
and spill rain like a leaky awning?
Atlanta is one exhausted sigh.

The repetition of the repetition of life—
I am unprepared, like everyone I suppose,
for the way the heart breaks daily.
Maybe it's best not to think about it.

I am exhausted from years of work.
My wife is exhausted from years of work.
Our daughter is worried about homework.
The dogs wag, expecting a Milkbone.

It's only Tuesday, and yet it's hard
to temper despair stopped at a red light
with my grotesque, wrinkled hand
in a death grip on the wheel.

Time and Distance

Again, the sidewalk stretches out ahead of me.
Again, I walk this path through the city.
On her last day of pre-school, our daughter
skipped the whole way—almost two miles,
in her red boots and her ladybug raincoat,
her street-side hand inside my wife's.
The morning storm had passed, steam rose
from the pavement like the remnants of a dream.
I followed behind, trying to hold it together.
Five years later, half her life, I am alone
walking to meet some friends for a beer.
They're at home, watching a movie without me.
I pass underneath the cherry blossom trees
and hear her voice through the time and distance:
"strawberry popcorn!" The image holds true.
The memory of that voice—the utter joy,
the "w" where the "r" should be—kneecaps me.
The leaves are falling. The fallen leaves,
a wet blanket over the city, slick and auburn.
I am always on the way to someplace else,
convinced there's always something better,
though I know this is goddamned lie.
Our daughter still skips, joyous as she goes—
she already knows so much more than me.

When It Rains

When you live beneath the trees
and it rains, it is possible
to go for a walk and stay bone dry.
When you live beneath the trees
and it has rained, it is possible
to come back drenched to the bone.

Love's Wishbone

> *And you are still my daughter.*
> W.D. Snodgrass

Two weeks ago, our daughter asked my wife
to show her how to shave her legs. I broke down
thinking not of the impossibility of her age,
but of the hot rush she must've felt if she saw
eyes linger over her body, maybe heard a snicker
from other girls who are not yet changing.
Broke down about how this will never end for her—
yet one more thing I cannot save her from.

Today, she turned ten, and all I can think about
is how we used to flank her as we walked,
her arms raised like a capital Y, one hand to each.
When there was a curb, or a puddle, she would leap
high as she could and swing, sure of nothing so much
as that we held her tight and would never let go.

To My Daughter in Her Sadness

You are my breath, and you are the absence
of my breath. My daughter, my sweet, sad girl,
I don't know what's wrong, and you won't tell me.
And you don't have to. You shift, turn away
lift the shade, the patchwork fields far below.
Somewhere over the heart of this country,
my daughter, I feel like I'm losing you.
It comes down on my chest like an anvil.
I can't breathe. If I could hold your sadness
within my lungs, suffocate it—I would.
But you are no longer my little girl,
and your pain must someday be all your own.
So, I reach out my hand, if nothing else.
You. You are not alone, my sad, sweet girl.

Buffet

She walks home, uphill, a stranger—
and yet, still half of me, still all of me.
Suddenly grown, no longer my little girl,
chatting with friends and laughing.
All the things I'll never know.

The afternoon sun is golden and cold;
the wind rises and buffets her hair.
She tucks it behind her ear, and *my God*,
my whole life there in a freezeframe.
Take my breath. Keep it forever.

Epilogue

Turn around. Turn away
from what you know to be,
from what you think has been.

Turn slowly on your heels;
survey the world rotating
across your narrow vision.

Turn it around now. Time
is running away. The apple
sags low on the bough.

Turn. Turn from your sacred
visions of second chances.
Dream, now, of your only future.

Acknowledgements

May 2023	"My Father In Waiting" accepted for publication in *After Happy Hour Review*.
October 2022	"Redemption" accepted for publication in *North Dakota Quarterly*.
April 2022	"The Broken Tent" accepted for publication in *The Pacific Review*.
February 2022	"Adult Swim," "Social Anxiety," "Taking a Nap With You," "How to Keep it Going," and "Summer Storm" published in *The Sandy River Review*.
February 2022	"The Heart Breaks Back" and "Grownup Magic" published in *Evening Street Review*.
January 2022	"A Dream of Leaving" accepted for publication in *Pulsar Poetry*.
January 2022	"Disappearances" published in *The MacGuffin*.
June 2021	"The Sense of Failure" and "The Halls of Churches" published in *Miller's Pond*.
May 2021	"The Selfishness of Men" published in *Nebo*.
January 2021	"The Mystery of Your Darkness" published in *Eclectica Magazine*.
January 2021	"Robin's Nest" published in *Ibbestson Street*.
October 2020	"Dancing in the Morning" accepted for publication in *The 1-70 Review*.
July 2020	"Flicker" published in *The Broadkill Review*.
June 2020	"Thoughts and Prayers" published in *The Comstock Review*.

About the Author

Robert Pfeiffer holds an MFA and PhD in creative writing from Georgia State University. He has published two previous collections of poetry with Plain View Press, *Bend, Break* (2011) and *The Inexhaustible Before* (2018). He has been publishing poetry for almost twenty years in international journals such as North Dakota Quarterly, Mudfish, The Haight Ashbury Literary Journal and The Flint Hills Review. He has recently relocated to the Seattle area with his wife and daughter.

www.ingramcontent.com/pod-product-compliance
Lightning Source LLC
Chambersburg PA
CBHW070111080526
44586CB00013B/1261